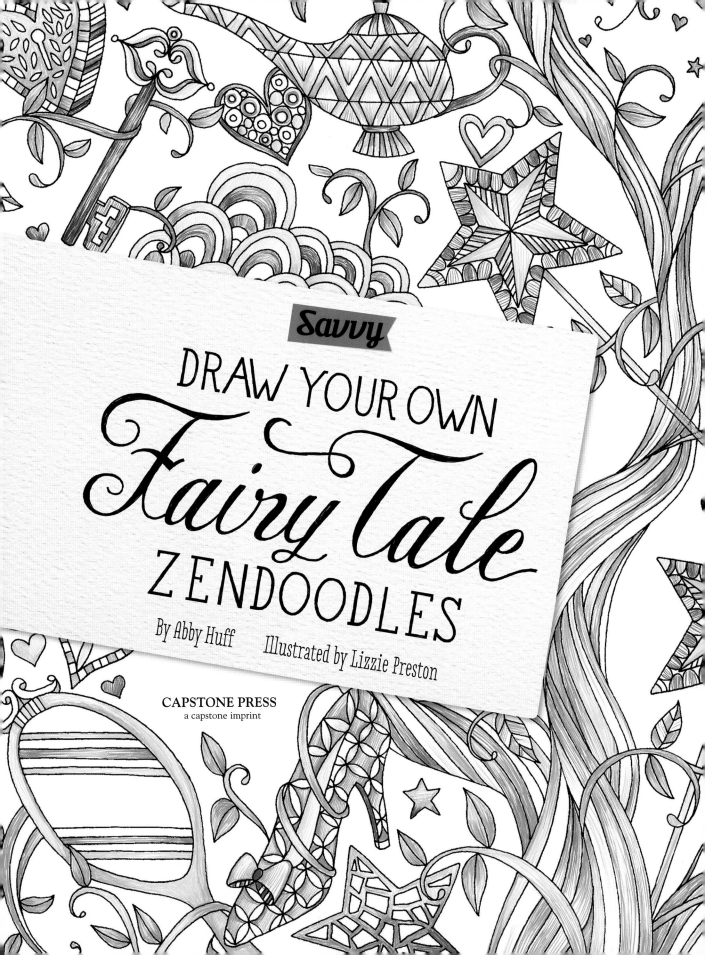

Savvy

DRAW YOUR OWN
Fairy Tale
ZENDOODLES

By Abby Huff   Illustrated by Lizzie Preston

CAPSTONE PRESS
a capstone imprint

Savvy Books are published by Capstone Press, a Capstone imprint
1710 Roe Crest Drive
North Mankato, Minnesota 56003
www.mycapstone.com

Library of Congress Cataloging-in-Publication Data
Names: Huff, Abby, 1991– author. | Preston, Lizzie, illustrator.
Title: Draw your own fairy tale zendoodles / by Abby Huff ; illustrated by Lizzie Preston.
Description: North Mankato, Minnesota : Capstone Press, 2017. | Series: Savvy.
 Draw your own zendoodles | Audience: Ages 9–13. | Audience: Grades 4 to 8.
Identifiers: LCCN 2016044395| ISBN 9781515748427 (library binding) | ISBN
 9781515748496 (ebook pdf)
Subjects: LCSH: Fantasy in art—Juvenile literature. | Fairy tales in art—Juvenile literature. |
 Drawing—Technique—Juvenile literature. | Handicraft for children—Juvenile literature.
Classification: LCC NC825.F25 H84 2017 | DDC 743/.87—dc23
LC record available at https://lccn.loc.gov/2016044395

Editorial Credits
Bobbie Nuytten, designer; Jo Miller, media researcher; Laura Manthe, premedia specialist

Image Credits
Capstone Studio: Karon Dubke, 7 (all), 18, 36, 44-47 (all), Shutterstock: Danyskar,
40 (gemstones), 42 (gemstone), Gelner Tivadar, 20, gresei, 14, ILeysen, 40 (diamond
shapes), Piotr Marcinski, 37, Robert_s, 24, Samuel Borges Photography, 38, StockLite,
39, Backgrounds: Shutterstock: aopsan, arigato, CCat82, donatas1205, happykanppy,
Lana Veshta, macknimal, Mikhail Pogosov, Nik Merkulov, Only background, Piotr Zajc,
Ratana21, redstone, siriak kaewgorn, Turbojet, Vadim Georgiev

Crafts created by Lori Blackwell and Tyson J. Schultz

Printed and bound in the United States of America.
010062S17

Table of Contents

Zendoodle Basics

Do you doodle? Then you can draw zendoodles — intricate designs built up from easy patterns. Simply clear your mind and get lost in creating curls, squiggles, and more. Don't stress about perfection. Just go with the flow. You'll be amazed at the beautiful (and relaxing) results. Here are some fundamentals to start you on your magical zendoodle journey.

Patterns

Zendoodles may look complicated, but they're created from basic patterns. Make patterns by repeating and layering different strokes and shapes. Using multiple designs in a zendoodle gives it its signature tangled style.

Shapes and Motifs

Small shapes and motifs (a fancy word for recurring forms and elements) can be used to help fill a zendoodle. Use teardrops, fans, circles, flowers, and more. Try drawing a cluster of shapes in your zendoodle or spread them out. Decorate them with dots, lines, or a pattern for an elaborate look.

Adding Patterns

Adding patterns is the most fun and calming part of the zendoodle process. There are two main methods. Try both to see which you like best.

Sectioned

Divide your drawing with lines.
Fill each section with a pattern.

Free-formed

Let your patterns overlap and run into each other. When you're done, it should be hard to tell where one pattern begins and another ends.

Object Zendoodles

Zendoodles don't have to resemble anything. You can simply fill a page with elegant patterns. Other times, it's fun to make your zendoodle into a recognizable object, like a heart or crown. When you're working with an object, try experimenting with these two methods.

Positive space

Draw inside the object. This is using the positive space — the space occupied by a subject. Decorate within the lines using adorable details and doodles.

Negative space

Draw around the object. This is using the negative space — the space around a subject. For maximum impact, don't add any details inside the object. Leave it completely blank for a striking graphic look.

Warm Up

Loosen your wrist and relax your mind. Get started with zigzags, squiggles, dots, curls, and more.

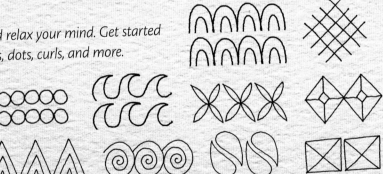

Zendoodle Tools & Materials

If you have a pencil and a scrap of paper, you're ready to zendoodle! But it can be fun to try out other supplies too. Here are a few essentials to keep in your toolbox.

Pencils

The most basic doodle tool. Try a mechanical pencil for consistently precise, even lines.

Paper

A page from your notebook can do in a pinch. For best results, use drawing or sketch paper. The thicker paper will hold up better to erasing and marking. Paper also comes in different textures. Generally, it'll be easier to doodle on a smooth surface.

Colors

Zendoodles are bold in black and white, but color adds a whole new dimension. Use colored pencils for a soft look. Try markers and colored pens for dramatic color. There are many options to choose from. Enjoy experimenting!

Pens

Pens are perfect for polished zendoodles. Splurge on drawing pens for smoother, high quality lines. Look for archival or pigment ink pens. The special ink won't smudge or fade, so it'll keep your design looking pretty.

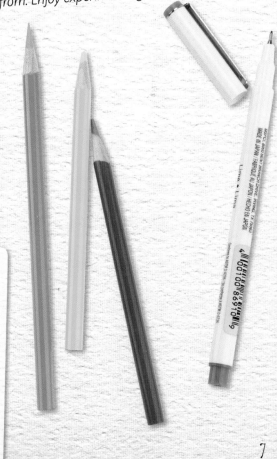

Quick and Easy Zendoodles

Not feeling confident in your drawing abilities? Want to start doodling right away? Head to **capstonekids.com**. There you can download sheets with blank outlines. Simply print the page and you're ready to go. Add exciting patterns and designs to make it your own.

Magic Mirror

Mirror, mirror, on the wall . . . it's obvious this zendoodle is the fairest of them all! Use angular lines to divide the mirror. It'll create a cool broken glass effect. Try layering rows of patterns to make an intricate frame.

Romantic Rose

A classic symbol of love goes from pretty to stunning. Stack dense patterns for a lush look. For lots of volume and drama, draw roses in full bloom. Choose a tight single bud for an elegant understatement.

Fairy Godmother's Wand

Cast a charm with this captivating zendoodle. Mix large teardrops and curls for a twirling burst of magic. Combine contrasting rounded and geometric designs for eye-catching variety. Sprinkle on twinkling stars to complete the enchantment.

Fairy Wings

Flutter it up with a pair of dainty fairy wings. Start with the provided
outlines or design your own. Model them after butterflies, dragonflies,
and other winged creatures. Decorate your fairy wings with delicate
flowers for a touch of whimsy.

Color It!

Turn your zendoodles into custom coloring pages.
If you drew in pencil, trace over your design with black
pen. A waterproof or archival quality pen is best. The
ink won't bleed if you color over it. Now you're ready
to start coloring with your favorite tool. Or, before you
color, make photocopies of your zendoodle. That way
you can color it again and again. You could even host
a coloring party for you and your friends!

15

Ancient Key

Let an old-fashioned key inspire your imagination. Does it unlock a door to a hidden garden? Perhaps it reveals lost treasure. Unwind as you decide the key's secret. Decorate it with easy petals and wavy lines for effortless charm.

Sparkling Glass Slipper

Bring this delicate footwear out of the storybook and into your sketchbook. Use a lavish design to decorate the main part of the slipper. The all-over look will create a rich, luxurious feel. Fill in the other areas with laid-back lines so the primary pattern can shine.

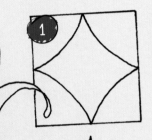
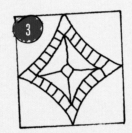
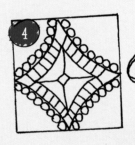

Creative Colored Pens

Freshen up your zendoodles and draw with colored pens! Switch out your black pen for bright neons, cool pastels, or sparkly glitter gel inks.

Here are a few ways to use your colored pens:

- Use one colored pen for the whole zendoodle.
- Pick a couple of colors. Doodle a large section in one color. Draw the next section in a new color. Alternate throughout the zendoodle.
- Draw the large shapes in your zendoodle using one color. Use other colors to make the patterns.
- Doodle in pen. Then take out colored pencils and color in your design. Choose hues similar to the pen for a coordinated look.

MADE IN JAPAN / FABRIQUE AU JAPON / HECHO EN JAPON

4 00100 86909 3

Teal • Sarcelle

Conforms to ASTM D-4236 / Se conforme à ASTM D-4236

Lovely Mermaid

Relax near the seaside with this aquatic beauty. Start with a graceful pose like the ones below. Give your mermaid zendoodle glamour and embellish the tail. Take your cue from ocean waves and use swirly, flowing patterns for a dreamy, underwater feel.

Organizing Patterns

Easily keep track of your favorite zendoodle patterns with note cards. Draw a sample of the completed design. If you want, include the step-by-step instructions. Punch a hole in the corner of your note card and slip it onto a loose-leaf binder ring. Flip through your cards when you need a bit of inspiration.

Climbing Beanstalk

Fee fi fo fum — no need to worry about giants here! Cover the page with this towering beanstalk zendoodle. Divide the plant into twisting sections. Try a new design in each area. Complete your drawing with curly twigs and little leaves.

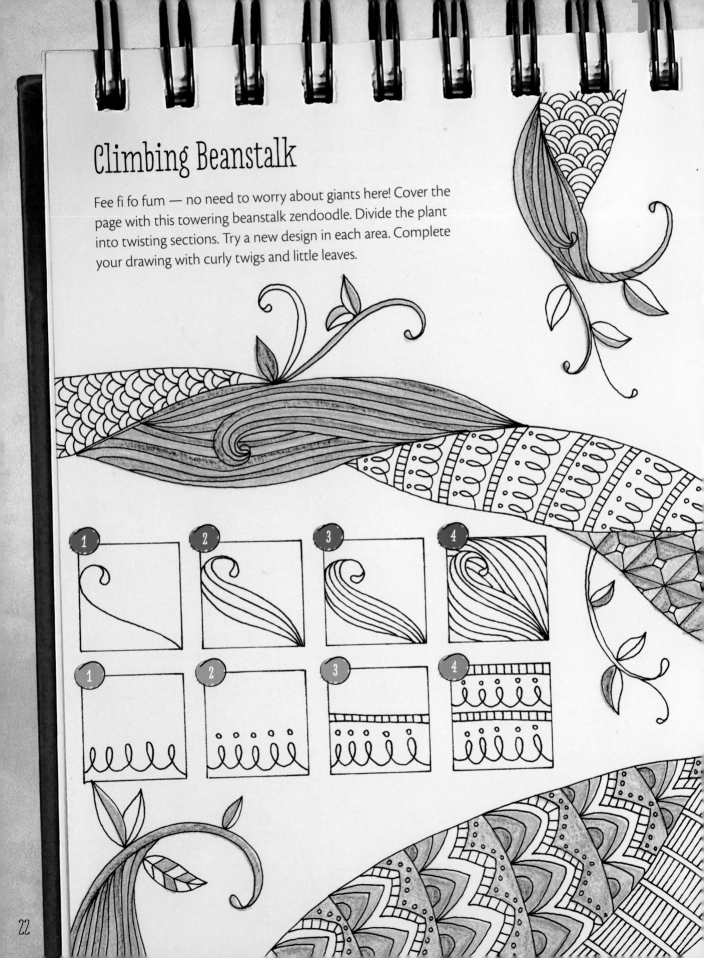

23

Castle Tower

Craft a picturesque fairy tale landscape using negative space. Draw the outline of a castle tower and doodle around it. Bring harmony to your zendoodle by focusing on a few larger shapes. Mandalas or flower-like designs create dazzling focal points.

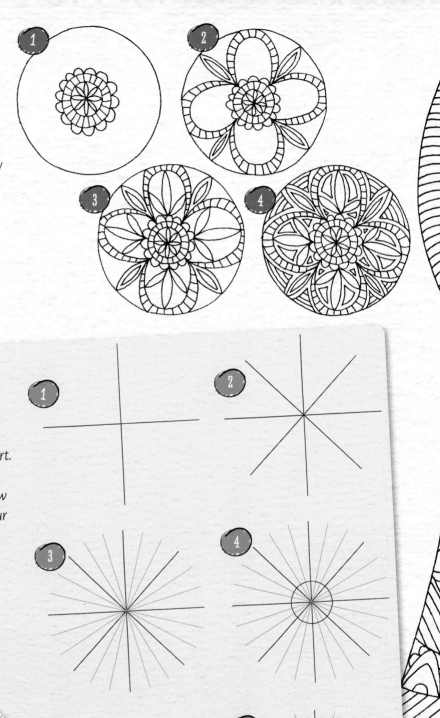

Making a Mandala

Construct a grid to keep your mandala balanced. Use a protractor to measure out even sections. Try 15 degrees to start. Then make layers using a compass. Place the needle in the center and draw circles with various diameters. Use your completed grid as a guide to creating symmetrical designs. Draw petals, triangles, and more in the sections, repeating them around the circle.

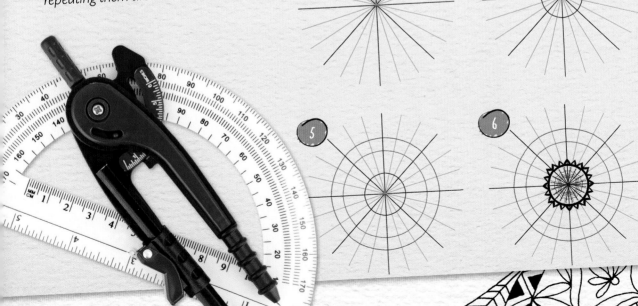

Fabled Unicorn

Capture the elegance of this noble creature with zendoodles.
Start by designing a large flower on the back, like a saddle.
Fill in the rest of the body with your favorite patterns. Color in a
rainbow mane and tail to make your unicorn truly spectacular.

True Love Heart

Create your own happily ever after. Make an adorable heart using two different methods. Fill the heart with romantic designs. Or doodle around it with a patchwork of patterns. Finish your heart with frilly, layered trim. Try out the three pretty looks below or design your own!

Mystical Genie Lamp

If you were granted three wishes, what would you ask for? Imagine your answers as you complete this swirling doodle. Keep your lamp simple and focus on the sweeping wave of enchanted smoke. Fill it with rows of patterns for a mesmerizing design.

Adding Watercolor

For a soft splash of color, try watercolors. Start with thick drawing or watercolor paper. With a large brush, apply a thin layer of water to the page. Load your brush with watercolor and paint onto the wet paper. Create the general shape of your design or try an abstract form. Dry completely before doodling over it with pencil or pen.

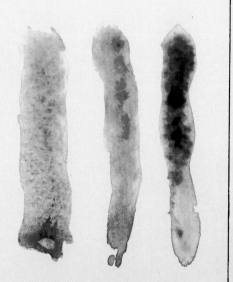

Princess Gown

Make a zendoodle dress fit for a royal ball. Scalloped shapes and curly patterns mimic the feel of sweet lace. Try this sweeping dress or draw your favorite dress silhouette. A puffy ball gown, sleek empire, or flirty mermaid style would all look gorgeous.

Legendary Dragon

If you're ready for a daring quest, draw this fearsome zendoodle. Diamond patterns make the dragon's skin look tough and strong. Design your own scale pattern to emphasize the dragon's reptilian nature.

Luscious Locks

Style a lovely princess hairdo. Be inspired by a
classic fairy tale princess or create your own
look. Braids, flowing tresses, tight curls, or a chic
updo are all perfect options for royal occasions.
Decorate each section of hair with regal patterns.
Try adding little sparkles or a cute flower for a
special accent.

Photo Fun

*Incorporate photographs into your drawing for a magical combination.
Carefully cut out a person from a magazine or from your own photos.
Paste your model onto paper and give her fantastic doodle locks. Or,
draw the hair first, cut it out, and paste it onto the photo.*

*You can also add a touch of zendoodle directly onto your photos. Use
permanent markers or paint pens to give yourself or your friends princess
hair. Try a set of fairy wings too, or embellish a pic with enchanting whirls
and dazzles. Customize your favorite memories however you'd like!*

Coronation Crown

Rule your kingdom with kindness — and style! Start with a traditional crown shape, like the ones shown below. Use a mixture of large and small designs to add drama. Angular patterns inspired by jewels will add a brilliant, noble glow.

Glittering Gems

Bring sophistication to your zendoodles with gems. Sketch one and make it gleam with color. Study pictures to see how color changes across a jewel. Or, try coloring a gradient. Go from dark to light. Use a white gel pen to add spots of shine along the edge. It'll help create a three-dimensional look.

For a quick and hassle-free approach, try stick-on jewels. Just peel off the gem and press it onto your drawing. Voilà! Now your zendoodle has some extra-special sparkle.

Get Crafty!

Zendoodles don't have to stay in your sketchbook. These fancy doodles are perfect for decorating and adding flair to everyday items. All you need is a little creativity. So if you're feeling artsy, try a variety of projects and crafts that'll showcase your zendoodles to the world. Be inspired to create your own DIY masterpiece — take your zendoodles off the page!

DIY Jewelry

Creating custom jewelry is a breeze with zendoodles and shrink plastic. Draw a complicated design or show off one chic pattern. Check the instructions on your shrink plastic for details on how much it'll shrink and for the bake time. Make sure to punch a hole in your piece before heating it. Display your finished charms on necklaces, bracelets, earrings, purse tags, and more!

Paint Chip Bookmarks

These colorful bookmarks are an easy afternoon craft. Grab a few paint chips in your favorite hues. You can usually find them wherever paint is sold. If needed, cut the paint chip to bookmark size. Then it's time to take out your pens! Add your favorite fairy tale zendoodles and decorations.

Glitzy Zendoodles

Prepare to be dazzled! All you really need is glitter glue and a small canvas. But if you want a colored background, brush on acrylic paint first. Then create your design. Go slow and steady with the glitter glue to get even lines. When it's all dry, hang and admire your glamorous art.

Deluxe Gift Box

Don't mess with wrapping paper. Use your doodle skills to beautify a gift box! Start with a basic paper box and make it one of a kind with all-over zendoodles. Try opaque pens like paint or pastel gel pens to make your decorations pop. Tie on a bow in a coordinating color for a fabulous finishing touch.

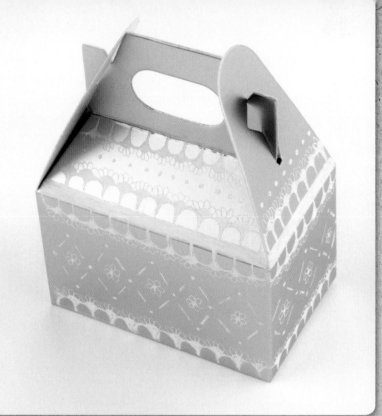

Fancy Origami Heart

Craft a special gift for a best friend or secret crush. Start with an easy origami heart in a rich color. If you need folding instructions, check out online tutorials or look at your local library. Adorn your folded model with zendoodle embellishments. Make it personal with a handwritten note on the back.

Artsy Manicure

Turn your nails into works of zendoodle art. Start with a base coat of your favorite color. Then add some flair! Nail art pens make adding details easy. You can also use an inexpensive fine-tip paintbrush to apply polish or acrylic paint. Top with a clear coat to protect your pretty artwork.

Embellished Jar

Make an everyday glass jar a showstopper. Use dimensional fabric paint to create your design. Try a pearly paint for subtle and sophisticated shine. Your jar will make a lovely pencil holder. Or turn it into a beautiful lamp by placing a small electronic candle inside for a warm glow.

Can't wait to draw your own zendoodles?

Visit **capstonekids.com** to download blank outlines. Simply print and start doodling. Add your own unique curls, twirls, and tangles!

Read More

Ames, Lee J. *Draw 50 Princesses: The Step-by-Step Way to Draw Snow White, Cinderella, Sleeping Beauty, and Many More....* Draw 50. New York: Watson-Guptill, 2012.

Corfee, Stephanie. *Twirly Girly Doodles.* Doodle with Attitude. North Mankato, Minn.: Capstone Press, 2016.

Marbaix, Jane. *Zentangle for Kids.* New York: Sterling Children's Books, 2015.

Internet Sites

FactHound offers a safe, fun way to find Internet sites related to this book. All of the sites on FactHound have been researched by our staff.

Here's all you do:
Visit www.facthound.com
Type in this code: 9781515748427